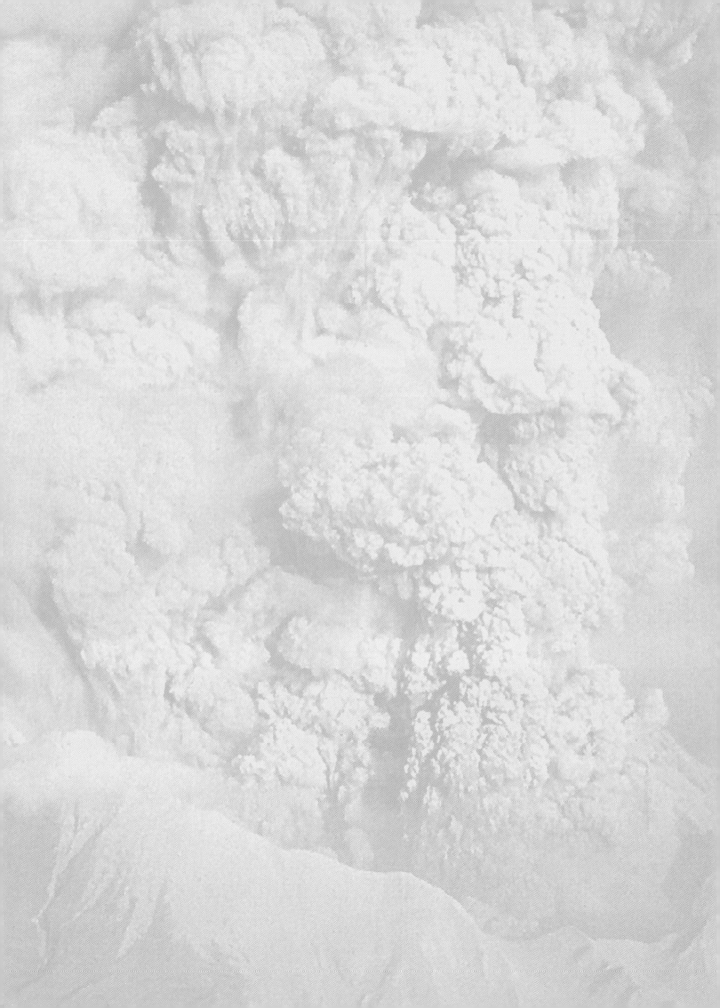

EARTH'S CHANGING LANDSCAPE

Earthquakes & Volcanoes

Chris Oxlade

First published in 2004 by Franklin Watts
Franklin Watts, 96 Leonard Street, London EC2A 4XD

Franklin Watts Australia
45–51 Huntley Street, Alexandria, NSW 2015
This edition published under license from Franklin Watts.

Series Editor: Sarah Peutrill; Series Designer: Simon Borrough; Art Director:
Jonathan Hair; Picture Researcher: Juliet Duff; Illustrations: Ian Thompson;
Series Consultant: Steve Watts, FRGS, Principal Lecturer in Geography
Education at the University of Sunderland

Published in the United States by Smart Apple Media
1980 Lookout Drive, North Mankato, Minnesota 56003

Library of Congress Cataloging-in-Publication Data

Oxlade, Chris.
Earthquakes & volcanoes / by Chris Oxlade.
p. cm. — (Earth's changing landscape)
Includes index.
ISBN 1-58340-479-1
1. Earthquakes—Juvenile literature. 2. Volcanoes—Juvenile literature. I. Title:
Earthquakes and volcanoes. II. Title. III. Series.

QE521.3.O95 2004
551.2—dc22   2004040185

9 8 7 6 5 4 3 2 1

Picture credits:
James Davis Travel Photography: 15, 23 left, 26.
Eye Ubiquitous: 21 CM Leask; 23 right Laurence Fordyce, 27 Paul Thompson;
28 Paul Seheult.
Geoscience Features: 7, 34 top.
Holt Studios International: 17 Dick Roberts; 34 bottom Rosie Mayer.
Frank Lane Picture Agency: 6, 36, 37.
Photodisc: 20.
Science Photo Library: 11 Simon Fraser; 18 Dr. Ian Robson; 19 Ray
Fairbanks; 41, 43 David Parker; 42 Jeremy Bishop.
Still Pictures: 9, 35 Edward Parker; 13 Jose Kalpers; 16 Martial Aquarone; 24
Steve Kaufman; 25 Nigel Dickinson; 29 Pierre Gleize; 31 Kevin Schafer; 40
Lineair.
Topfoto: 22, 38, 39.

Front Cover: Still Pictures/Otto Hahn.

CONTENTS

For most of us, the landscape of Earth's surface seems permanent, solid, and safe. But over millions of years, the landscape has been changed dramatically by earthquakes and volcanic eruptions. These events have built mountain ranges, created chains of islands, and destroyed major cities.

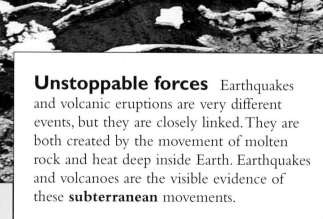

These buildings were destroyed by a landslide that was caused by a massive earthquake in Alaska in 1964.

Unstoppable forces Earthquakes and volcanic eruptions are very different events, but they are closely linked. They are both created by the movement of molten rock and heat deep inside Earth. Earthquakes and volcanoes are the visible evidence of these **subterranean** movements.

**Follow it through:
subterranean movement**

Movement of molten rock inside Earth

Earthquakes shake Earth

Volcanoes erupt

Effects on the landscape

Most earthquakes and volcanoes affect only a relatively small part of the landscape. On a local scale, they are very dramatic events, but on a global scale, they are minor. However, over millions of years, the subterranean movements that cause earthquakes and volcanic eruptions have changed the appearance of the entire planet.

Earthquakes cause the ground to shake. In most cases, when the shaking stops, the landscape is left unchanged. But strong earthquakes can crack the ground, trigger landslides and mudslides, create huge waves at sea, and knock down buildings.

Volcanoes have a greater effect on the landscape than earthquakes. Much of Earth's surface is covered with rock from volcanoes. Volcanoes build mountains and islands thousands of feet high, cover the ground with **lava** and **ash**, create devastating mud flows, bury and burn buildings, and even change the world's **climate**.

Case study: Heimaey

In January 1973, a crack appeared on the island of Heimaey near Iceland.

Volcanic eruption

Fountains of lava poured from the crack. Cinders rained down, forming huge cones, and lava flowed across the landscape, forming new rocks and enlarging the island by about a quarter of its original size. The eruption lasted five months. The town of Vestmannaeyjar was evacuated, and a third of its houses were destroyed, but people moved back afterward.

Ground cracks

Lava and ash erupt

Landslides occur; giant waves form at sea

New mountains and islands form; mud flows occur

The landscape is changed

INSIDE EARTH

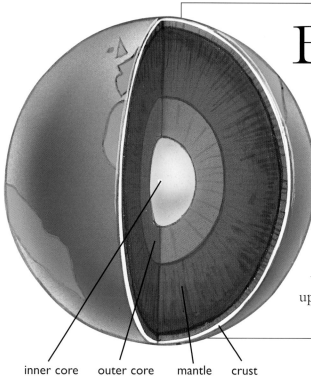

Before we can understand how earthquakes and volcanoes change Earth's landscape, we need to know about the structure of Earth.

Inside In the center of Earth is the core, which is made mostly of iron. This is divided into the inner core and outer core. Around the core is the **mantle**. On top of the mantle, there is a very thin layer called the **crust** that makes up Earth's surface.

inner core   outer core   mantle   crust

Under the surface The top layers of the mantle are called the asthenosphere and the lithosphere. They are made of hot, partly-molten rock. These layers are responsible for creating earthquakes and volcanoes.

The crust, made of solid rock, rests on top of the lithosphere. The part that makes the continents, called continental crust, is about 31 miles (50 km) thick. The crust under the oceans, called ocean crust, is about three miles (5 km) thick.

The huge pressure from the crust stops the incredibly hot rock in the mantle from turning to liquid.

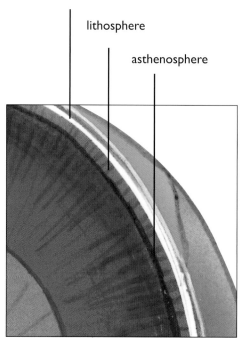

crust

lithosphere

asthenosphere

Follow it through: plate movement

Heat is created in Earth's core

Heat creates currents in semi-molten rock in the mantle

The cracked crust

The crust and the upper part of the lithosphere are cracked into huge pieces called **tectonic plates**. These plates float on top of the semi-molten rock underneath. They move at about the same speed as human fingernails grow. Scientists think that tectonic plates move because of the slow, swirling movements of semi-molten rock deep in the mantle.

Continental drift

The movements of the tectonic plates mean that some continents are moving apart, and some are moving toward each other. This process, known as continental drift, has been going on for hundreds of millions of years. Two hundred million years ago, when dinosaurs lived on Earth, there was just one huge continent. Plate movements have split it into the continents we know today.

In the process, new oceans have been created, old oceans have disappeared, and new mountain ranges, such as the Andes, have been built as continents have collided. Continental drift will carry on for millions of years to come, gradually changing the look of Earth's surface.

Take it further

The supercontinent of 200 million years ago was called Pangaea.

◆ Find a map of Pangaea.
◆ Copy the outlines of North America, South America, Africa, India, the rest of Asia, Europe, Antarctica, and Australia from an atlas.
◆ Can you fit these shapes together to make the shape of Pangaea?

The great mountain chain of the Andes was built by volcanic activity caused by movements of the tectonic plates.

Currents flow under the crust

Currents make the tectonic plates move slowly

Some continents move apart, and some move toward each other

PLATE BOUNDARIES

The line where two tectonic plates meet is called a **boundary**. Most earthquakes and volcanic activity happen near these boundaries. There are three main types of plate boundary: plates moving apart, plates moving toward each other, and plates sliding past each other.

A slice through the crust showing a constructive boundary and destructive boundaries

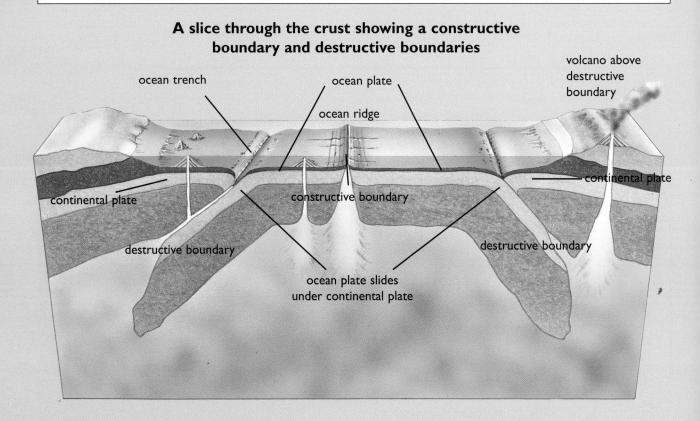

ocean trench

ocean plate

ocean ridge

volcano above destructive boundary

continental plate

continental plate

constructive boundary

destructive boundary

destructive boundary

ocean plate slides under continental plate

Destructive boundaries

A place where the edges of two plates are moving toward each other is called a **destructive boundary**, also known as a subduction zone. When two plates meet, there are different results depending on whether the plates form a continent or are under the ocean.

When a continental plate and an ocean plate meet, the ocean plate slides underneath the continental plate. It plunges into the mantle and melts, forming new **magma**.

When two ocean plates meet, one plate slides under the other and melts. When two continental plates collide, the plates crumple into each other, pushing up huge mountain ranges. The Himalayas were made when the Indian plate collided with the Asian plate.

Constructive boundaries

A place where the edges of two plates are moving away from each other is called a **constructive boundary**. As the plates move apart, magma—which is molten rock from the mantle—flows into the gap. The magma cools and hardens to form a new crust.

The **Mid-Atlantic Ridge** is a constructive boundary that runs north-south on the ocean floor of the Atlantic. The two plates are gradually moving apart, so the Atlantic is gradually getting wider. The Great Rift Valley in Africa is also a constructive boundary.

Take it further

Find a map of the ocean floor in an atlas.

◆ Can you identify the Mid-Atlantic Ridge (a constructive boundary)?
◆ Which island has formed over this spreading ridge?
◆ Look for other spreading ridges under other oceans.

A constructive boundary between two continental plates in Iceland. The line shows were the two plates are slowly moving apart.

Conservative boundaries

In some places, the edges of two plates slide past each other without moving apart or toward each other. No rock is made or destroyed, so this sort of boundary is called a **conservative boundary**. However, the movements can destroy the edges of the plates.

WHERE VOLCANOES FORM

A volcano is simply a place where magma leaks out through a hole or crack in Earth's crust. Most volcanoes form along constructive boundaries or destructive boundaries between tectonic plates, but a few form far from plate boundaries.

Volcanoes at destructive boundaries

When an ocean plate plunges under another plate, the ocean plate rubs against the plate above and gets hot. The rock melts, making magma under the upper plate. This pool of magma forces its way up through weak points in the crust. This creates a line of volcanoes parallel to the boundary but off to one side in the upper plate.

Over millions of years, volcanoes create mountain ranges such as the Andes, or chains of islands such as the Aleutian Islands in the north Pacific. Most of the world's volcanoes occur at destructive boundaries.

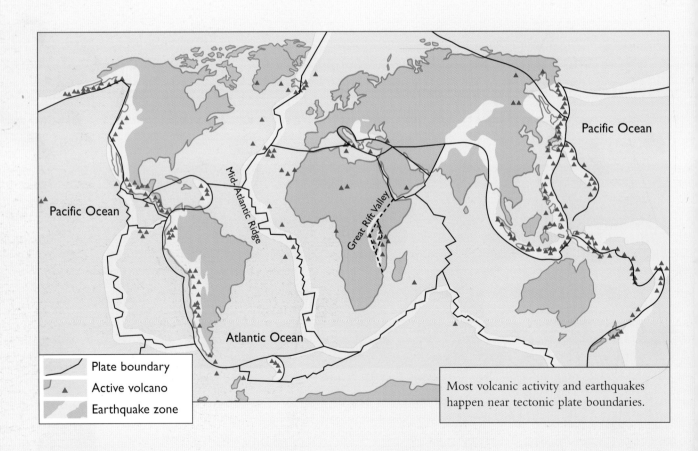

Pacific Ocean

Mid-Atlantic Ridge

Great Rift Valley

Pacific Ocean

Atlantic Ocean

Plate boundary
Active volcano
Earthquake zone

Most volcanic activity and earthquakes happen near tectonic plate boundaries.

Follow it through: volcanic eruption

An ocean plate and a continental plate meet

The ocean plate sinks under the continental plate

The ocean plate experiences friction and pressure

The Ring of Fire   Nearly all the way around the Pacific Ocean is a line of destructive plate boundaries where ocean plates slide under continental plates and other ocean plates. These boundaries have created a circle of volcanoes around the rim of the Pacific known as the Ring of Fire. It runs along the west coasts of South America and North America, through the Aleutian Islands, Japan, the Philippines, and New Zealand.

Volcanoes at constructive boundaries   Volcanoes also form along constructive boundaries. As the two plates at the boundary move apart, magma wells up from underneath to fill the gap and form volcanoes. The Mid-Atlantic Ridge that runs along the floor of the Atlantic Ocean can be thought of as a continuous volcano that is thousands of miles long.

Hot-spot volcanoes   Volcanoes also **erupt** thousands of miles away from tectonic plate boundaries. It is thought that these eruptions occur over places in the mantle that are hotter than normal. Magma from these **hot spots** forces its way through the crust above.

All over the world   There are about 500 volcanoes in the world that have erupted in the recent past, and, on average, 25 volcanoes erupt every year. A few have been erupting ever since people can remember.

Nyamulgaria in Congo, Africa, is a hot-spot volcano.

| The ocean plate melts, forming magma | Magma forces its way toward the surface | Magma breaks through the continental plate | A volcano erupts at the surface |

INSIDE A VOLCANO

Volcanoes come in many different shapes and sizes. The simplest volcano is just a crack in the ground that leaks flowing magma. The biggest volcanoes are immense heaps of rock that can be as big as mountains. They are built from layers of material that have been ejected during previous eruptions.

ash cloud

vent

side vent

lava flow

crust

magma chamber

Volcano parts The diagram shows the parts of a composite volcano (*see page 19*). Magma forces its way from the **magma chamber**, through the crust, then up the center of the volcano through a hole in the top called the **vent**. A wide hole in the top of a volcano is also known as a **crater**. Magma sometimes comes out of side vents, too.

Eruption products Magma is a mixture of molten rock and gases such as carbon dioxide and steam. High pressure on the magma when it is deep underground keeps the gas dissolved despite the high temperature. But when the magma rises through a volcano's vent, the pressure is released and the gas turns into bubbles. The gas comes out of the vent along with bits of molten rock called lava.

If small lumps of lava cool before they land, they form small pieces of rock called **cinders**. Larger pieces are called volcanic bombs. Lava that lands while it is still molten forms red-hot liquid on the ground. In explosive eruptions, the rock in magma can be turned into tiny fragments that cool quickly to form ash.

Take it further

Shake a bottle of soda pop. Hold the bottle over the sink and make sure the top is pointing away from your face. Unscrew the cap very slowly and watch the liquid carefully.

◆ Why do you think bubbles appear in the liquid?
◆ How does this relate to magma moving to a volcano's vent?

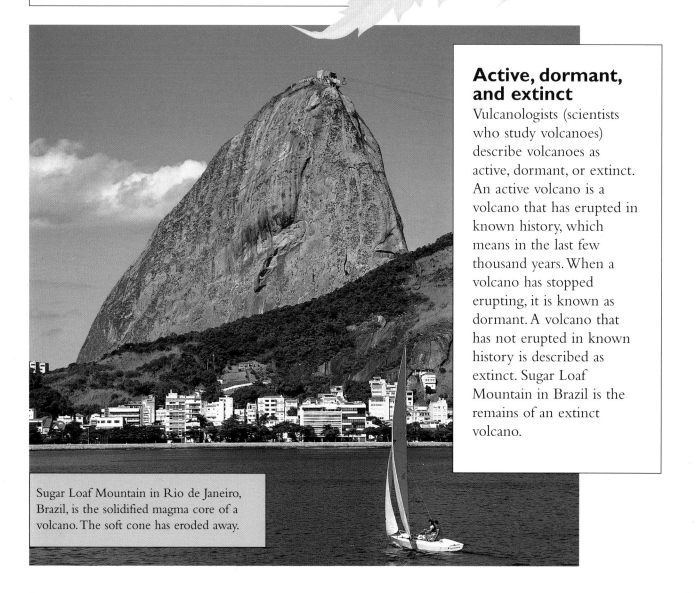

Sugar Loaf Mountain in Rio de Janeiro, Brazil, is the solidified magma core of a volcano. The soft cone has eroded away.

Active, dormant, and extinct

Vulcanologists (scientists who study volcanoes) describe volcanoes as active, dormant, or extinct. An active volcano is a volcano that has erupted in known history, which means in the last few thousand years. When a volcano has stopped erupting, it is known as dormant. A volcano that has not erupted in known history is described as extinct. Sugar Loaf Mountain in Brazil is the remains of an extinct volcano.

NEW ROCKS

Volcanoes create new rocks that form part of the landscape. This is an important stage in the process called the rock cycle, in which new rocks are continually formed, and old rocks are broken down and destroyed.

New rocks Molten rock from the magma released by the volcano cools and solidifies to form new rock. This often builds into mountains and mountain ranges (*see page 18*). Eruptions under the sea form a new ocean crust and even entire islands (*see page 20*).

Gentle eruptions The volcanoes that erupt at constructive boundaries and over hot spots tend to be gentle when compared to the violent eruptions of some volcanoes. In these gentler eruptions, lava comes out of the volcanoes in fountains. Such eruptions are known as Hawaiian and Strombolian eruptions after the islands where they were first studied.

    The lava is driven out of the vent by gases released from the magma. It falls to the ground and forms pools. If the ground is sloping, the lava flows away from the vent in a river called a lava flow.

An eruption at Stromboli, near Sicily, Italy. The red-hot lava will cool to form new rock.

Follow it through: rock cycle

Lava flows from the volcano

Lava cools to form new igneous rock

Rock is eroded

Temperature or pressure changes

Rock formation As soon as lava leaves a volcano vent, it begins to cool. However, a deep lava flow can travel dozens of miles before it cools enough to stop flowing. Liquid lava can flow at up to 12.5 miles (20 km) per hour on steep slopes. When the lava cools fully, it forms igneous rock. Examples of igneous rocks from volcanoes are basalt, granite, andesite, and pumice stone.

The other types of rock, sedimentary and metamorphic, are both ultimately formed from igneous rock. Sedimentary rock, such as sandstone and limestone, is created through compressed fragments of other rock and shells. Metamorphic rock is changed from its original state into a different rock due to changes in temperature and pressure.

Lava shapes Small flows of very hot lava form rock with a surface like coiled rope. This is called *pahoehoe* lava. Large flows of cooler lava form rock with a sharp, jumbled surface. This is called *aa* (*see page* 7). *Pahoehoe* and *aa* are Hawaiian words.

A flow of *pahoehoe* lava formed this rock called basalt about 18,000 years ago.

Case study: the Deccan Traps, India

Sometimes lava flows spread out to form extensive lava fields that cover the landscape. One of the world's biggest lava fields is the Deccan Traps in India. It is also one of the largest volcanic features on Earth.

Thick layer

The Deccan Traps were formed about 65 million years ago when lava flows created a layer of basalt that was 1.2 miles (2,000 m) thick across an area of 193,000 square miles (500,000 sq km). Much of the basalt has been eroded away. Scientists think gases and ash from the eruption may have contributed to the extinction of the dinosaurs.

Layers of sediment form that become sedimentary rock

Rock becomes metamorphic rock

Millions of years of rock movements

Rock moves deep underground

Rock melts to form magma

NEW MOUNTAINS

Lava and ash from volcanoes build new hills and mountains that can be thousands of feet high. A new volcanic hill or mountain may take millions of years to form, or it can be created in just a few months or even a few days. The sort of volcanic hill or mountain formed depends on the type of eruption.

The Mauna Loa volcano in Hawaii is a shield volcano.

Shield volcanoes When very hot, liquid lava is ejected from a volcano and spreads quickly across the landscape, it forms thin layers of new rock. Each eruption creates a new layer of rock on top of the previous one. Gradually, a wide dome of rock is built. This sort of volcano is known as a shield volcano because it is shaped like a curved shield lying on the ground. It looks like an upside-down dinner plate. The Mauna Loa volcano in Hawaii is an example of a shield volcano.

Follow it through: composite volcanoes

Magma moves upward from under the crust

Pressure on the magma is reduced

Gas blasts lava into the air

A series of ash and cinder cones have been formed on the island of Maui, Hawaii.

Cinder cones

Some volcanoes spew magma that is about half gas and half lava. The gas expands as the magma rises to the surface. It throws small lumps of gas-filled lava high into the air. The lumps cool before they land and form cinders. When the cinders land, they form a cone-shaped hill with a wide crater in the top. This sort of volcano is called a cinder cone. Cinder cones often form in clusters and on the sides of larger volcanoes.

Composite volcanoes

Magma that contains a high percentage of gas and only a little lava tends to be ejected explosively, forming small particles of ash. A composite volcano, also known as a stratovolcano, is made of layers of this ash with layers of lava in between. Some of these volcanoes form perfect cones that are thousands of feet high, such as Mount Fuji, Japan. These volcanoes form over destructive boundaries.

Case study: Paricutín, a new Mexican mountain

On February 20, 1943, Mexican farmer Dionisio Pulido noticed small earth tremors, and the ground in his fields felt warm. Both were the first signs of a new volcano.

Eruption

The next day, a crack opened in the ground and an eruption began. Ash soon began to pile into a cone, and lava flowed from the top and down the sides. By July, a composite cone volcano 980 feet (300 m) high dominated the landscape. Dionisio's village, Paricutín, had been buried. The eruption stopped in 1952 when the cone had reached a height of 1,380 feet (420 m).

| Lava cools to form ash | Ash piles up to form a cone | Fresh lava flows over the cone | More ash falls on the lava flows | A composite cone is built |

ISLAND BUILDING

There are many more volcanoes under the ocean than there are on the continents. Underwater eruptions happen at constructive boundaries such as the Mid-Atlantic Ridge, at destructive boundaries where two ocean plates meet, and over hot spots under the ocean. Most of these volcanoes are never seen, but some grow large enough to break the surface and form new islands.

Islands in constructive zones At constructive zones, magma comes up between plates that are spreading apart. It cools very quickly to form rounded heaps of lava called pillow lava. In a few places, these eruptions are large enough to build entire islands. For example, Iceland was formed from lava flowing from the Mid-Atlantic Ridge.

Hot-spot islands On volcanic hot spots under the ocean floor, magma can force its way through the crust and form a shield volcano on the sea bed. If the eruption continues long enough, the tip of the volcano eventually forms a new island.

The island of Hawaii is the tip of a sea bed volcano. It is more than 5.5 miles (9 km) high and 370 miles (600 km) wide at its base. One of the volcanoes on Hawaii, Mauna Loa, is the world's most active volcano.

To the northwest of Hawaii is a line of islands formed from extinct volcanoes. It is thought that these also formed over the same hot spot as Hawaii.

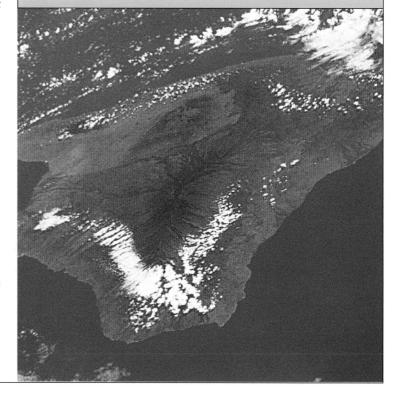

The island of Hawaii as seen from space. The whole island is made of material spewed from its volcanoes.

Follow it through: island chains

Hot magma under an ocean plate forms a hot spot

A volcano begins to form on the ocean floor

Eventually, a volcano breaks the surface

The caldera of Deception Island forms a perfect natural harbor used by visiting cruise ships.

Islands at destructive boundaries

Chains of volcanic islands form next to destructive boundaries. For example, an 1,800-mile (3000-km) long chain of islands runs through the Pacific Ocean south of Japan. This is to the west of where the Pacific plate slides under the Philippines plate. To the east of the islands is a trench in the ocean floor, up to 6.8 miles (11 km) deep, where the Pacific plate dips down.

Case study: Deception Island

Deception Island is an active volcano in the South Shetland Islands, Antarctica. It was formed over a destructive boundary.

Caldera formation

Sometime in the past, Deception Island had a volcanic mountain in its center. Then, there was a catastrophic eruption that blew the mountain apart. The center of the volcano collapsed into the magma chamber underneath, and the sea rushed in to form a **caldera** (see page 23). There have been minor eruptions during the last hundred years.

| A new island is formed | An ocean plate moves | The eruption stops | A new volcano begins to form in a different place on the sea bed | A chain of islands is formed |

EXPLOSIVE VOLCANOES

Eruptions of volcanoes over destructive boundaries are often extremely violent and spectacular. Instead of forming new rock or building new mountains, these volcanoes can destroy themselves in huge explosions. They also change the landscape for many miles around. Explosive eruptions such as this are called Plinian eruptions after Pliny, a Roman who saw the eruption of Vesuvius, Italy, in A.D. 79.

Building up pressure The magma formed at destructive boundaries is thick and stiff, and it contains a high percentage of gases. After an eruption in a volcano above a destructive boundary, the volcano's vent can become plugged with magma, preventing more magma from escaping.

Over many years, perhaps hundreds of years, more magma is forced into the magma chamber underneath the volcano. The pressure on the plug increases. Eventually, the pressure becomes so large that the magma bursts out.

An example of a Plinian eruption. This is Mount Pinatubo in the Philippines at the height of its eruption in 1991.

Exploding out With the pressure on the magma released, the gases dissolved in it explode. The huge forces blow the lava in the magma into tiny pieces that cool to form ash. The top of the volcano cone can be blown apart, too. Explosive eruptions continue until the pressure in the magma chamber is reduced.

Calderas When the eruptions die down, the top of the volcano can collapse into the empty magma chamber, forming a huge crater called a caldera. This often fills with water and a caldera lake is created. Crater Lake in Oregon is a famous lake-filled caldera. It is about 6.2 miles (10 km) wide and 3,200 feet (1 km) deep.

A caldera created by the eruption of Mount Pinatubo.

Rebuilding the cone After an explosive eruption destroys the top of a volcano, the volcano often begins to rebuild itself. Small eruptions of lava emerge from cracks in the volcano and form domes in the top of the volcano and down its sides.

The landscape around Mount St. Helens was devastated after its eruption.

Case study: Mount St. Helens, Washington

Mount St. Helens in the Cascade Mountains is a destructive boundary volcano.

Eruption

Mount St. Helens had been dormant for more than 100 years when it erupted in 1980. The eruption began with ash and rock flying into the air. Then, the north side of the mountain began to bulge. On May 18, the pressure inside caused the mountainside to collapse, and there was a massive explosion of trapped gas.

Widespread destruction

Trees up to 18 miles (30 km) away were broken like matchsticks. Valleys, lakes, and rivers were filled with mud and debris, and 59 people were killed, as well as vast numbers of animals, birds, and fish. The top 1,300 feet (400 m) of the mountain was blown away. A new cone is forming inside the vast crater that was left.

VOLCANIC ASH

The effect of a volcanic eruption is not limited to the volcano itself. Explosive eruptions can change the landscape for hundreds of miles around or, sometimes, Earth's entire surface.

Ash clouds Explosive eruptions create vast clouds of volcanic ash. The ash is carried into the air by hot gases rising upward, just as smoke rises from a bonfire. Volcanic ash clouds can rise as far as 31 miles (50 km) into the atmosphere. The ash gradually falls back to the ground, covering it in a thick, grey blanket. This layer of ash is not light, like dust, but is as heavy as rock.

Mount Augustine in Alaska is a typical explosive volcano. In 1986, eruptions continued for several weeks, spewing a permanent ash cloud 2.8 miles (4.5 km) high. Occasional huge explosions pushed the ash cloud as high as 7.6 miles (12.2 km). The ash was thrown upward from the explosions and carried still higher by the hot gases.

Ash exploding high into the air from Mount Augustine volcano.

Follow it through: climate change

An explosive volcano creates clouds of ash

Ash is carried into the stratosphere by rising hot gas

High-level winds move the ash

Climate change   The biggest explosive eruptions send ash into the upper atmosphere, where it is carried around Earth by currents of air called the jet stream. This ash reduces the sunlight that can reach Earth's surface. The eruption in 1815 of volcano Tambora in Indonesia is thought to have blocked so much light that crops failed all over the world.

Thick layers of ash found in sediments seem to show that there have been even more catastrophic eruptions in the distant past. These eruptions may have caused long-term cooling of the atmosphere, changing the world's climate, which, in turn, may have changed the pattern of plant and animal life. Eruptions may have even caused **mass extinction** of some types of wildlife.

Take it further

Search the Internet for videos of pyroclastic flows.

◆ Can you see how the heavy ash cloud flows down the hillside like an avalanche?
◆ Try to find examples filmed at night that show the glowing ash and rocks carried by the flow.

Pyroclastic flows   Sometimes the ash cloud is so thick that rising gas cannot carry it upward and away from the volcano. Instead, it collapses and flows down the volcano's slopes like an avalanche. This is called a **pyroclastic flow**. It is made of scorching hot gas and ash. Pyroclastic flows can reach speeds of more than 90 miles (150 km) per hour, destroying everything in their path.

Central Luzon in the Philippines. The explosion of Mount Pinatubo covered the landscape in thick, white ash. The volcano also emitted sulphur gases that may have contributed to climate change and damage to the ozone layer.

| A layer of ash is carried around Earth | Ash blocks sunlight from reaching the surface | Less heat reaches the surface | The atmosphere cools | The world's climates are affected |

Mixing water with volcanoes can have devastating effects. Water and volcanic ash form rivers of mud, and explosive eruptions on islands can create huge waves at sea. Where water seeps into volcanically active ground, however, it creates interesting effects such as **hot springs**.

Mud flowing after the eruption of Mount Pinatubo, Philippines.

Mud flows

Ash deposits from volcanoes often mix with rain water or melted snow from a volcano's summit to create mud flows known as **lahars**. These sweep downhill into river valleys and follow the path of the rivers. The mud is incredibly dense. It carries away anything in its path, including trees, bridges, and buildings. When the flow finally comes to a stop, the mud sets like a layer of concrete over the landscape.

Case study 1: Nevado del Ruiz mud slide, Columbia

In 1985, Nevado del Ruiz, a snow-capped volcano in the Andes in northern Columbia, began to erupt. The eruption was quite small, but the ash from pyroclastic flows melted snow and ice, forming lahars.

Devastating effects

The lahars flowed at speeds of up to 37 miles (60 km) per hour. They eroded soil and loose rock and stripped vegetation. With the rock, vegetation, and water from river channels, the lahars grew in size, becoming as thick as 160 feet (50 m) in some areas. Two and a half hours after the start of the eruption, one of the lahars reached the town of Armero, located 46 miles (74 km) from the explosion crater. In a few minutes, the town was buried forever under many feet of mud, along with 22,000 of its inhabitants—around three-quarters of the population.

Volcano waves

Explosive eruptions of island volcanoes can leave vast craters in the sea. The sea rushes to fill the crater, creating monster waves called **tsunamis** (*see page 37*). In 1883, the Indonesian island of Krakatoa exploded, leaving a crater 950 feet (290 m) deep in the sea floor. The tsunamis created were up to 131 feet (40 m) high and killed about 36,000 people on nearby islands.

Follow it through: mud flows

Volcano erupts

Heat from the lava melts snow and ice

Heavy rain falls

Water mixes with ash to make mud

Volcanic features   There are often peculiar landscape features on and around volcanoes. The rocks under the ground are heated by magma close by. Hot springs often flow from these hot rocks. In a few places, water boils quickly underground and the steam throws columns of water back to the surface, forming geysers. Hot rock also forms pools of boiling volcanic mud.

A multi-colored steaming mud pool at Waiotapu Thermal Park, North Island, New Zealand.

Case study 2: Loki melting ice cap, Iceland

In 1996, a volcano called Loki erupted under Iceland's **ice cap**. The heat melted ice so that water collected under the ice cap. This eventually lifted and released the water in a massive flood.

Flood effects

Two bridges and a section of road 6.2 miles (10 km) long were destroyed by the flood. River beds were totally changed. More than 100 million tons of sediment were carried to the ocean, causing the shoreline to move by several hundred feet in some areas. The floods even carried boulders the size of houses out to the sea.

Torrents of mud flow into river valleys

Mud flows onto flood plains

Mud slows, stops, and sets hard

EFFECTS ON THE HUMAN LANDSCAPE

All of the effects volcanoes bring to the natural landscape also affect features created by humans. For example, lava flows bury farmland, burn buildings, and block roads. Thick ash deposits bury homes, and mud flows carry away bridges and destroy towns.

Rice terraces thrive on volcanic ash at Mount Agung in Bali, Indonesia.

Living with volcanoes

Despite this, about one-tenth of the world's population (about 600 million people) live in cities, towns, and villages where they are at risk from eruptions.

The people most likely to be at risk are farmers in less economically developed countries. Crops grow very well near volcanoes because the soil—formed from lava and volcanic ash—is rich in minerals. In some places, farmers even build terraced fields on the steep volcano slopes.

Towns and cities have also been built near volcanoes, often because of lack of space elsewhere. Generally, people accept the risks of living near volcanoes because the chances of being hurt are small and the advantages outweigh the risks.

With the increasing number of people on Earth, more people will be forced to move into dangerous volcanic regions.

Permanent and temporary changes

Sometimes, places are permanently changed by volcanic eruptions and their effects. For example, lava and mud flows can completely bury farmland and communities. People are then forced to move on. But ash can often be removed, lava flows can be cleared from roads, and people can return to their homes and lives. A few years later, there may be no sign that an eruption ever took place.

The city of Quito, Ecuador, lies in a valley surrounded by volcanoes. It regularly receives a covering of volcanic ash. In 2002, an eruption of the volcano El Reventador dropped two inches (5 cm) of ash on the city. Local people are well-prepared for these events. They formed teams to collect and carry away the ash, and the city was working again within a few days.

Human effects

Gentle eruptions are not normally dangerous because lava flows quite slowly, and there is plenty of time to escape. But violent eruptions can be deadly. People close to volcanoes can be caught in ash falls, pyroclastic flows, mudslides, and tsunamis.

When the composite volcano Vesuvius erupted in Italy in A.D. 79, it buried the towns of Herculaneum and Pompeii under many feet of ash. When it erupted again in 1944, the ruins of Pompeii were buried under ash once again—but this was only temporary.

Plaster casts of the people overcome by volcanic ash in the streets of Pompeii in A.D. 79.

Case study: Mount Pinatubo, Philippines

The Philippines is a less economically developed country with a relatively high population. In 1991, Mount Pinatubo erupted after being dormant for 400 years.

Widespread effects

Earth tremors were felt in April, and the mountain's sides began to swell. A series of explosions in June sent up an ash cloud 12 miles (20 km) high. Ash fell to the ground, turning farmland for 31 miles (50 km) around into wasteland and burying more than 40,000 homes. Despite mass evacuations, thousands of people died in collapsed homes, pyroclastic flows, and mudslides (see *page 26*).

An earthquake happens when rocks in Earth's crust move suddenly, shaking Earth's surface. The shaking causes changes to the landscape such as cracks in the ground, landslides, and, if strong enough, it can destroy buildings. About 10,000 earthquakes are felt every year, but most are so small that they are detected only by sensitive instruments.

Slipping plates

1 Two plates catch as they grind against each other.

Slipping plates Like volcanoes, most earthquakes happen on or near the boundaries between Earth's tectonic plates (*see map page 12*).

Tectonic plates grind past each other rather than sliding smoothly. As one plate moves against the other, it can catch. The edges of the plates stop moving, but pressure gradually builds as the rest of the plate keeps going—bending, stretching, and squeezing the rocks at the edges.

At some point, the pressure becomes too large and the catch releases. The plates move suddenly, releasing the pressure, and then catch again. This sudden jerk causes an earthquake.

2 Pressure builds until eventually the catch releases, causing an earthquake.

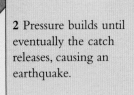

Follow it through: earthquakes

Tectonic plates move past each other

The surfaces of the plate edges stop moving

The plates keep moving

Destructive and conservative quakes

Major earthquakes happen at both destructive and conservative boundaries. At destructive boundaries, earthquakes can come from almost any depth, and the movements of the rocks are often large.

At conservative boundaries, the movement of the plates past each other fractures the two plate edges, creating a band of **faults**—cracks in rock—up to 62 miles (100 km) across. Earthquakes that happen at conservative boundaries tend to come from near the surface.

Surface evidence

Some faults are deep below ground, but some are near the surface. Some go right through the crust. Often, the rocks on each side of a fault have moved up, down, or sideways.

The San Andreas fault in California is on a conservative boundary. There, the two plates are actually both moving in the same direction, but one is moving faster than the other. This causes the potential for earthquakes.

The San Andreas fault runs for about 590 miles (950 km) along the coast of California.

More earthquake zones

Earthquakes are also caused by the movement of magma at constructive boundaries, under volcanoes, and where continental plates collide and push up mountain ranges.

They can also happen far from plate boundaries, in places we would not expect them. Such earthquakes are probably caused by faults formed millions of years ago.

The British Isles are thousands of miles from any plate boundary, but they still experience minor earthquakes. In 2002, an earthquake centered in the Midlands was felt up to 62 miles (100 km) around. It was caused by movement in an ancient fault deep underground.

Pressure builds on rocks at the plate edges

Rocks bend, compact, and stretch

The catch releases

Rocks spring back into shape

An earthquake is triggered

EARTHQUAKE WAVES

The point in Earth's crust where two plates slip and create an earthquake is called the **focus**. Energy released from pressurized rocks radiates out from the focus in shock waves called **seismic waves**.

Body waves The seismic waves that spread through Earth from the focus are called body waves. They radiate in all directions—both toward the surface and deeper into Earth. They travel many miles every second.

Two types of body waves are created—primary and secondary. Primary waves move in waves of compression and tension, like sound passing through the air. Secondary waves move like a wave along a string, shaking the rocks from side to side.

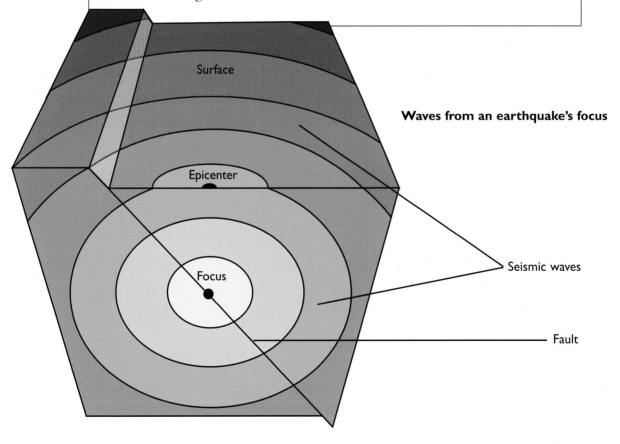

Surface

Waves from an earthquake's focus

Epicenter

Focus

Seismic waves

Fault

Follow it through: seismic waves

Rocks spring back into shape as a boundary or fault slips at the focus

The movement causes body seismic waves

Surface waves When body waves reach the surface, they create waves that travel across the surface. There are two types of these surface waves: Rayleigh waves and Love waves, named after the scientists who first described them. Seismic waves make the landscape move up and down and from side to side as they pass, but normally leave it undamaged after they have gone.

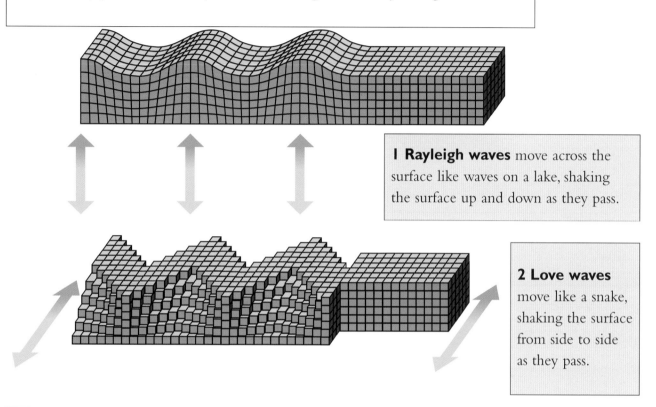

I Rayleigh waves move across the surface like waves on a lake, shaking the surface up and down as they pass.

2 Love waves move like a snake, shaking the surface from side to side as they pass.

Earthquake scales The magnitude of an earthquake is a measure of the energy it releases. It is measured on the Richter Scale. On this scale, a small earthquake might measure 3, a strong quake 6, and a massive quake 8 or more. Going up the scale by one represents an increase in energy of 10 times.

The intensity of an earthquake is a measure of its strength based on the changes it causes to the landscape. It is normally measured on the Modified Mercalli Scale. On this scale, level 1 is a minor tremor that causes no damage, and level 12 is total devastation.

Weakening waves As seismic waves spread out from the focus, they get weaker, just as a sound gets quieter further from the source. So, although an earthquake can have only one magnitude, its intensity reduces as the distance from the focus increases.

The epicenter The greatest intensity is at the **epicenter**—the point on the surface directly above the focus. A medium magnitude earthquake with a shallow focus can be more intense and cause more damage than one with a high magnitude and a deep focus.

| Body waves reach the surface | Surface waves are triggered | Surface waves spread from the epicenter | Body waves and surface waves shake the ground |

During an earthquake, seismic waves shake the ground. There can also be small earthquakes before and after the main earthquake (called foreshocks and aftershocks). But this shaking is only temporary. What are the lasting effects of earthquakes on the natural landscape?

Surface upheaval Strong seismic waves can rip layers of weak rock apart, creating cracks in the surface. These are normally just hairline cracks rather than wide chasms.

If the two sides of a fault move in an earthquake, the ground on one side can move up or down compared to the other. This creates a new step in the land, called a scarp.

Sideways (or transverse) movements of faults rip the surface. These can be seen by a line of disturbed ground, or sections of road or fences that have moved out of line. An earthquake in Montana in 1959 caused timber and road damage estimated at $11 million.

Streets cracked by ground waves during the 1959 Montana earthquake.

A raised beach in Cornwall, UK.

Raised beaches

Earthquakes can make the ground rise or fall by several feet, or be tilted. These changes are not always easy to see. Evidence for them comes from raised and sunken beaches. A raised beach is an eroded shoreline that has been lifted above sea level.

Backward rivers Tilting ground can also make rivers change their course. In the early 1800s, an earthquake in Tennessee made the Mississippi River flow backward, filling depressions in the land to create new lakes.

Landslides The shaking caused by earthquakes is often enough to make unstable hillsides, mountain slopes, and cliffs fall downward, creating a landslide. In a large landslide, soil and rock accelerate down the slope, sweeping away everything in their path. Landslides can fill valleys, creating temporary dams that release flood water when they collapse. Earthquakes also trigger avalanches on snow slopes.

A strong earthquake in Ecuador in 1987 caused landslides that dumped millions of tons of soil into the Amazon River.

Case study: Peruvian landslide

In 1970, an earthquake with a magnitude of 7.7 struck off the coast of Peru.

Wide effects

Towns and villages 40 miles (65 km) along the coast were badly damaged, but the worst devastation was 40 miles (65 km) inland, in the heart of the Andes. Here, the earthquake had triggered an immense landslide of snow and rock. It reached 173 miles (280 km) per hour before spreading out 33 feet (10 m) thick on the valley floor. The towns of Yungay and Ranrahirca were buried, and 50,000 people lost their lives.

EARTHQUAKES AND WATER

The combination of an earthquake and a landscape containing water can cause major problems. Ground that appears to be perfectly solid turns to quicksand. The shaking creates damaging waves on lakes and, worse still, destructive waves at sea.

Waterlogged soil

Land such as flood plains, coastal flats, old lake beds, and reclaimed land is normally made of sediment layers such as silt and sand. In millions of years, these will become new sedimentary rock, but, until then, they are soft and often waterlogged. Shaking these sediments has a strange effect on them. The water moves to the surface, creating quicksand. This is known as liquefaction. When the shaking stops, the water sinks down and the ground turns solid again.

The effects of liquefaction
Liquefaction can have devastating consequences. Heavy objects resting on the ground sink downward. Lighter things underground, such as underground pipes and even human bones, float upward to the surface. If the ground is on a slope, the hillside turns to mud and forms a mudslide. New springs can emerge from the ground. Occasionally, water is ejected in fountains through weak spots in the surface. The water carries sand that forms volcano-like cones several feet high.

During the 1964 Alaskan earthquake, soft clay liquefied and slid downhill.

Follow it through: tsunamis

An earthquake occurs under the ocean

The ocean floor moves up or down

Water above moves up or down

Tsunamis

If an earthquake happens in rocks under a sea or ocean, the shock waves disturb the water. If the ocean floor also falls or rises suddenly, the water falls or rises, too. These movements create huge waves called tsunamis that travel across the ocean. Landslides on coasts of continental shelves can trigger waves as well.

A tsunami starts off very low, with a long wavelength (a large distance between each crest) and travels up to 430 miles (700 km) per hour. People on ships in mid-ocean do not even notice it passing.

But when the tsunami reaches shallow water, it slows down, its wavelength reduces, and its height grows. Strong tsunamis can grow as high as a 10-story building. When a tsunami hits the shore, it crashes inland, carrying boats and buildings with it.

Take it further

Investigate how liquefaction works.

◆ Put five tablespoons of cornflour into a bowl.
◆ Slowly add water until the mixture is a thick, sticky paste. Let the paste settle. Press the surface. Does it resist?
◆ Now shake your finger quickly from side to side as you press. Does the paste turn to a liquid? This is how the ground liquefies in an earthquake.

A ship washed up with debris on the port of Seward, Alaska, after a tsunami.

Waves spread from the epicenter

Waves travel fast across the deep ocean

Waves get higher as they reach the shore

Water rushes inland

The landscape is flooded

COLLAPSING BUILDINGS

Seismologists (scientists who study earthquakes) often say that earthquakes do not kill people—buildings do. The vast majority of people killed and injured in earthquakes are trapped in buildings that topple or crumble because of the ground shaking underneath. In major earthquakes, urban landscapes can be completely destroyed. Even buildings that stay standing may have to be later demolished because of structural damage.

Earthquake damage in Kobe.

Why buildings collapse

As seismic waves pass a point on the ground, the ground moves violently up and down and from side to side. Up and down movements do not tend to damage buildings because buildings are designed to carry vertical forces. But sideways shaking can make all types of buildings collapse.

The walls of simple mud-brick houses are shaken to bits. Even concrete buildings can collapse like card houses.

The waves move up the building, cracking the joints between the concrete walls and floors, and the floors collapse on top of each other into a jumbled heap of concrete, brick, and dust.

Case study: the Kobe earthquake, Japan

In January 1995, Kobe was hit by an earthquake measuring 7.2 on the Richter Scale.

Earthquake damage
More than 6,000 people died and nearly 200,000 buildings collapsed or were damaged. Most modern buildings survived. A long section of an overpass toppled sideways, and subway tunnels collapsed. The worst affected area was in the center of Kobe along the main docks and port. This area is built on soft and easily moved rocks, and the port itself is built on reclaimed land. There, the ground liquefied (see page 36) so buildings fell sideways.

Fire damage
Fires from broken gas pipes caused many of the deaths and much of the damage. The collapse of electricity and telephone lines meant that it was difficult for the firefighters to find out where the fires were. It took over two days to control the fires, by which time it is estimated that over 7,000 buildings were damaged, and 500 people were killed by fire.

Follow it through: collapsing buildings

Waves spread

The ground shakes from side to side

Buildings shake from side to side

Buildings that survive

Whether a building survives depends on its structure, its height, and how quickly the ground shakes. Tall buildings often survive better than buildings of medium height, even though they might sway wildly. Some tall buildings have collapsed because their tops have collided with each other.

Earthquake proofing

Buildings can be designed to withstand earthquakes. In most cities at risk from earthquakes, new buildings must be earthquake proof. Making a building earthquake resistant is often as simple as making it stronger. For example, adding extra steel reinforcement to a concrete building can stop the concrete from crumbling. It may not prevent a building from being damaged beyond repair, but it may stop it from collapsing completely. A building can also be isolated from the ground to minimize the shaking. One way of achieving this is by mounting it on rubber foundations.

Road damage after an earthquake in 1994 in Los Angeles, California.

Damage to infrastructure

It is not just houses and office buildings that are damaged by earthquakes. Infrastructure such as roads, railroads, bridges, communications, and services can be damaged, too. Broken gas pipes start fires and broken water mains cut off the water supplies needed to fight them.

Walls of brick buildings are shaken apart

The structure of concrete buildings is broken

Buildings collapse

People are trapped under rubble or concrete slabs

LIVING WITH EARTHQUAKES

Changes to urban landscapes caused by earthquakes are normally only temporary. After victims are found, rubble is quickly cleared away, buildings rebuilt, and services restored. Only in ancient times were earthquake-damaged cities completely abandoned.

Tons of rubble must be painstakingly lifted in the search for earthquake survivors. This is a scene in Turkey in 1999.

Rich and poor

Cleaning up after earthquakes, however, is an expensive process, and it happens more quickly in more economically developed countries than less economically developed countries, where people may have to live in temporary accommodations for many years.

About 30,000 people were killed and 500,000 more made homeless by a quake that hit the Indian state of Gujarat in 2001. Despite international aid, thousands of the homeless were still living in tented camps two years later.

Earthquake risks Hundreds of millions of people live in earthquake zones, many of them in major cities such as San Francisco, Tokyo, and Istanbul. All of these cities were hit by severe earthquakes in the 20th century. It is almost certain that they will be hit again this century, but they have been rebuilt and continue to grow. It is simply impractical to relocate these cities, and most people have little choice but to live in them.

Learning by mistakes It is important for structural engineers to learn what goes wrong with buildings during earthquakes. They try to work out why buildings collapse so that poor designs can be avoided in the future.

Unfortunately, this does not always happen. For example, after a Turkish earthquake in 1999, engineers discovered that the builders of collapsed concrete tower blocks had taken shortcuts to save money on materials, making the buildings dangerously weak.

Be prepared We cannot stop earthquakes from happening, but we can reduce the risks to people by making sure that the inhabitants, authorities, and emergency services are prepared. This can be as simple as telling people to take shelter under tables during an earthquake.

In urban areas of more economically developed countries, plans can be put into action within minutes. But in remote areas of less economically developed countries, victims may have to fend for themselves for days until help arrives.

Take it further

Look at a political map in an atlas.

◆ Compare the map to the earthquake location map on page 12.
◆ Can you identify major cities that are at risk from earthquakes?

Children practice an earthquake drill in California. The building is earthquake-resistant, with shatter-proof windows and an earthquake alarm. Computers and bookcases are bolted down to stop them from falling.

EARTHQUAKE AND VOLCANO RESEARCH

Research into volcanoes (called vulcanology) and earthquakes (called seismology) is very important. Scientists try to understand why earthquakes and volcanic eruptions happen and predict when they will occur. This is difficult because the causes of earthquakes and volcanoes are deep underground. However, monitoring tiny changes to the landscape can help.

A vulcanologist using a camera next to a lava flow on Mount Etna, on the Italian island of Sicily, Italy.

Monitoring volcanoes A volcano gives plenty of clues that it is about to erupt. For example, there are small earth tremors as magma begins to move, the ground swells as pressure builds up, and particular gases—such as sulphur dioxide—are emitted.

Vulcanologists use instruments such as seismometers to monitor these signs. Examining rock and ash around a volcano tells vulcanologists when previous eruptions happened and how long they lasted. Using this data, they get an idea of the pattern of eruptions from a volcano, which helps with long-term predictions.

Monitoring earthquakes

Earthquakes are much harder to predict than volcanic eruptions. They tend to happen suddenly, without warning.

Seismologists use seismographs to monitor earthquakes, and other instruments to measure movements across faults. Readings tell them whether plate boundaries and rocks on each side of faults are moving past each other smoothly. If the movement stops for longer than normal, an earthquake is likely to follow—but it could be the next day or the next year.

Other signs of an impending earthquake are movements of water under the ground and changes in the electrical resistance of the rocks.

There is a network of seismographs all over the world. They are very sensitive and can detect earthquakes on the other side of the world. Data from them helps scientists to understand how seismic waves travel.

Warning and evacuation

If a volcanic eruption seems imminent, people at risk can be evacuated, although it is normally hard to predict an exact eruption time. This was successful in the case of the Mount Pinatubo eruption in 1991 and eruptions on Hawaii, where it was even possible to tell which vent magma would flow from.

There is normally no time to give earthquake warnings, and evacuating big cities in just a few hours is impractical anyway. However, seismologists can say if a large earthquake is likely in the following years, and maps are drawn to show which areas of cities are most at risk from building collapse.

In conclusion

Earthquakes and volcanoes are driven by huge forces produced deep inside Earth. They have created sweeping changes to our natural landscape over millions of years and will continue to do so.

We cannot stop earthquakes and volcanic eruptions from happening, but with research, predictions, and warnings, we may be able to reduce both the changes they make to the human landscape, and the number of people who lose their lives.

Case study: the Neptune Project

The Neptune Project is a collaboration between the U.S. and Canada to study the plates beneath the oceans.

Ocean observatory

The project involves the installation of 1,860 miles (3,000 km) of fiber-optic cables linked to sensors across a plate under the Pacific Ocean. These will send real-time information about our changing planet via the internet to shore-based users. It will mean that the changes associated with earthquakes will be continually monitored and help to prevent future disasters.

A technician checks a creepmeter at Parkfield in Central California. Creepmeters can detect ground movements of only minute distances and can often give the first warning of an earthquake.

GLOSSARY

Ash	Tiny particles of rock spewed out of a volcano.
Boundary	A place where two tectonic plates meet.
Caldera	A huge crater, often full of water, formed when a volcano collapses into its magma chamber.
Cinders	Small pieces of rock formed when lumps of lava ejected from a volcano cool before they land.
Climate	The pattern of weather in a place over a long period of time.
Conservative boundary	A plate boundary where two plates slide past each other.
Constructive boundary	A plate boundary where two plates move apart, and new crust is formed.
Crater	A dish-shaped hole in the top of a volcano.
Crust	The rocky top layer of Earth.
Destructive boundary	A plate boundary where two plates move toward each other, and crust is destroyed.
Epicenter	The point on Earth's surface directly above the focus of an earthquake.
Erupt	To eject lava or ash from a volcano into the air.
Faults	Cracks in Earth's crust.
Focus	The point in Earth where an earthquake occurs.
Friction	The force that tries to stop two touching surfaces from sliding past each other.
Hot spots	Spots in a tectonic plate where magma forces its way through to the surface.
Hot springs	Places where water heated by hot underground rocks flows out of the ground.
Ice cap	A thick, permanent layer of ice on the top of a high mountain range or at the poles.
Lahars	Mud flows made of volcanic ash and water.
Lava	Hot, molten rock that comes from a volcano.
Magma	A mixture of molten rock and gases under Earth's crust.
Magma chamber	A huge cavern full of magma under a volcano.
Mantle	The thick layer of hot rocks between Earth's core and crust.
Mass extinction	An event in which thousands of species of animal are killed off at the same time.

Mid-Atlantic Ridge	A line of underwater mountains along a constructive boundary in the center of the Atlantic Ocean.
Pyroclastic flow	An avalanche of hot gas and ash that flows down the side of a volcano.
Seismic waves	Waves that spread through Earth and across the surface from the focus of an earthquake.
Subterranean	Under the ground.
Tectonic plates	The huge sections of Earth's crust that float on the mantle.
Tsunamis	Giant ocean waves caused by an undersea earthquake, a landslide, or volcanic explosion.
Vent	A hole in a volcano from where lava or ash is emitted.

FURTHER INFORMATION

United States Geological Survey
The USGS site has the latest news on earthquakes around the world. Features an excellent education section.

www.earthquake.usgs.gov

Savage Earth
This Web site for the PBS program series *Savage Earth* includes information, maps, and graphic animations on earthquakes, volcanoes, and tsunamis.

www.pfs.org/wnet/savageearth/

Discovery Channel
The Discovery Channel earthquake site includes an earthquake simulator.

http://tlc.discovery.com/convergence/quakes/interactives/makeaquake.html

Volcano World
Dedicated volcano Web site. Features a variety of volcano photos and videos, reports, and stories.

www.volcanoworld.org

The Stromboli Web site
Excellent site mainly about the Stromboli volcano in Italy. Also features other Italian volcanoes, including Etna. Links to volcano Web cams.

www.educeth.ch/stromboli/

Monserrat Volcano Observatory
Latest news, pictures, and research from the Soufriere Hills volcano that has devastated the island of Monserrat in the Caribbean since 1995.

www.mvo.ms

INDEX

6-9